Wild Predators!

Deadly Reptiles

Heinemann Library
Chicago, Illinois

Andrew Solway

Design: David Poole and Calcium
Illustrations: Geoff Ward
Picture Research: Maria Joannou and Catherine
  Bevan
Production: Camilla Smith

Originated by Ambassador Litho Ltd
Printed and bound in China by
South China Printing Company.

09 08 07 06 05
10 9 8 7 6 5 4 3 2 1

**Library of Congress Cataloging-in-
Publication Data**
Solway, Andrew.
  Deadly reptiles / Andrew Solway.
    p. cm. -- (Wild predators)
  Includes bibliographical references and index.
  ISBN 1-4034-6568-1 (hc) -- ISBN 1-4034-
6574-6 (pb)
  1. Reptiles--Juvenile literature. I. Title. II.
Series.

  QL644.2.S695 2004
  597.9--dc22
                                    2004018571

Acknowledgments
The author and publisher are grateful to the
following for permission to reproduce copyright
material:
Alamy Images p. **38**; AP Photo p. **25 bottom**
(Rick Bowmer); Ardea p. **5 bottom** (Francois
Gohier), **12** (Masahiro Lijima), **16** (M Watson),
26 (M D England), **33** (John Mason), **37 bottom**
(John Daniels), **39** (Tom & Pat Leeson); Corbis p.
5 top (Sally A Morgan/Ecoscene), **19 bottom**
(Jim Zuckerman), **22**, **30** (Martin Harvey/Gallo
Images), **43 top** (Eric & David Hosking); Digital
Stock pp. **24**, **25 top**; Ecoscene p. **13**; FLPA pp.
6 (R Austing), **8** (Larry West), **10** (Minden
Pictures), **11** (Panda Photo), **15 top** (Gerard
Lacz), **18** (Minden Pictures), **19 top** (Wendy
Dennis), **21** (Terry Whittaker), **27 top** (Roger
Tidman), **31** (David Hosking), **34** (Gerard Lacz),
35 (Gerard Lacz), **36** (High Clark), **37 top**
(Jurgen & Christine Sohns), **40** (Foto Natura), **41**
top (D Ellinmger/Foto Natura); Getty Images p.
32 (Imagebank/Jonathan & Angela Scott); Nature
Picture Library pp. **17** (D Kjaer), **23** (Michael
Pitts); NHPA pp. **15 bottom** (Daniel Heuclin), **41**
bottom (Daniel Heuclin), **42** (Daniel Heuclin);
Oxford Scientific Films pp. **7** (David Fox), **9** (Zig
Leszcynski), **14** (Zig Leszcynski), **20** (Des & Jen
Bartlett), **27 middle**, **28** (Zig Leszcynski), **29**
(Mark Deeble & Victoria Stone), **43 bottom**
(Breck P Kent).

Cover photograph of the American crocodile,
Crocodylus actus, reproduced with permission of
Alamy/Mark Newman.

The publisher would like to thank Peter
Heathcote of the Exotic Animal Welfare Trust for
his assistance in the preparation of this book.

Every effort has been made to contact copyright
holders of any material reproduced in this book.
Any omissions will be rectified in subsequent
printings if notice is given to the publisher.

Contents

Scaly Hunters

Acrocodile lurks in a water hole ready to grab an unsuspecting drinker. A leatherback turtle cruises the ocean snapping up jellyfish. A chameleon on a tree branch flips out its tongue to catch a passing insect.

These are all reptile hunters, and they hunt in different ways. The one thing they have in common is their scaly skin. Crocodiles, alligators, turtles, and lizards are all reptiles. (Snakes are reptiles, too, but they appear in the another book in this series, *Killer Snakes*). Crocodiles and alligators are well known as fearsome predators, but there are lizards that can kill an animal as large as an adult buffalo, and there are even dangerous turtles!

Cold-blooded?

Reptiles are known as cold-blooded animals, but their blood is not actually cold. What this means is that they are not warm-blooded animals, like birds and mammals.

Warm-blooded animals can keep their bodies at the same temperature, even when the weather is cold, by using energy from food to make heat. Cold-blooded animals cannot do this. If the weather is cold, they cool down, and if it is hot, they warm up.

Because they are cold-blooded, reptiles cannot survive as well in cold areas as mammals and birds can, so most reptiles are found in warmer lands. However, there are also advantages to being cold-blooded. Making heat takes energy, so cold-blooded animals

Mammals are hairy, birds have feathers, and amphibians are smooth, but reptiles are scaly. Their scales are not separate like fish scales, but are joined together by thin skin.

Reptiles can often manage to keep their bodies warm by the way they behave. For instance, lizards often rest in burrows overnight, then bask in the sun to warm up in the morning.

need less energy and less food than warm-blooded ones. Some reptiles can survive for months without eating. This is a great advantage in harsh environments, such as deserts, where food is scarce.

Eggs with shells

Most reptiles lay eggs with either hard or leathery shells. A few lizards and snakes give birth to live young, rather than laying eggs. Reptiles do not sit on their eggs to keep them warm, as birds do. Instead they either bury them or cover them with a pile of leaves and plants. Most reptiles leave their eggs to hatch by themselves, but female crocodiles guard their eggs.

Age of the reptiles

For millions of years, reptiles were the most successful animals on the planet. From about 200 million years ago until 65 million years ago, the dominant land reptiles were dinosaurs. They ranged in size from huge animals over 98 feet (30 meters) long to small, fierce predators the size of chickens.

Other reptiles also dominated the air and the oceans. Pterosaurs with leathery wings flew through the air, and dolphin-like ichthyosaurs roamed the seas.

The skeleton of a *Triceratops* dinosaur shows the animal's size.

Turtles and Tortoises

In a shallow stream in Trinidad, a matamata turtle lies still, waiting. Its flattened shell looks like a piece of bark, and its head looks like a dead leaf. Under its chin it has strange folds of skin. A small fish swims by, and the ripples it creates make these folds of skin wobble. The matamata senses the ripples. It lunges forwards with its long neck and suddenly opens its large mouth. It sucks in water, and the fish gets sucked in with it.

Turtles and tortoises are known as chelonians. They are easy to recognize because of their protective shells. The majority of chelonians are called turtles, but land-living turtles are often called tortoises. Chelonians live in a wide variety of habitats, from dry deserts to the open ocean.

A horny shell

A turtle's tough shell is part of its body, not a separate structure. The shell has an outer covering of horny material. This is a modified version of the turtle's scaly skin. Underneath is a layer of bony plates that are fused (joined) to the turtle's ribs and spine. The top part of the shell is called the carapace, while the bottom part is the plastron.

The shell is a turtle's portable armor. When danger threatens, most turtles can pull their legs and head right into the shell.

There are two main groups of turtles. Hidden-necked turtles, such as this box turtle, bend their neck in an S-shape to pull in their head, while side-necked turtles bend their head to one side.

Meat-eating turtles

Turtles are unlikely predators. They are slow movers, and they do not even have any teeth! Most tortoises (land-living turtles) are vegetarians, but a few hunt prey that is even slower-moving than themselves, such as snails, slugs, and worms.

In water, some turtles are not slow like their land-based relatives. They have streamlined shells, and their legs are flattened into flippers that help them swim at great speeds. The fastest swimmers are sea turtles that use their large front flippers to glide through the water.

Many turtle predators do not need to be speedy to catch their prey. Like the matamata, they stay in one place and ambush their victims. The matamata eats fairly small prey, but turtles that eat larger animals have a powerful beak with razor-sharp edges that can slice through flesh.

The longest lives

Land-living turtles live longer than any other vertebrates (animals with backbones), including humans. Some turtles kept in captivity have lived for more than 150 years, and one turtle is known to have lived 200 years! In the wild, a marked eastern box turtle is known to have survived 138 years.

Snapping Turtle

A fish swimming in the shallows of the Mississippi River sees something pink wiggling in the water that looks like a nice, juicy worm. It swims closer to investigate, but that is the last thing it ever does. The pink thing is not a worm; it is part of an alligator snapping turtle's tongue. As the fish grabs what it thinks is a worm, the snapper's jaws close around it.

There are two species of snapping turtle, which live only in eastern North America. The common snapping turtle grows to nearly 20 inches (50 centimeters), while the alligator snapper can be 30 inches (75 centimeters) or longer. Both species have a long tail and a large head.

Common snapping turtle

Common snapping turtles are found from Canada to Central America, in shallow streams or lakes. They live as far north as southern Canada, where the water is too cold for most turtles to survive.

Common snapping turtles hunt at night. They hide on the bottom of the stream or lake and wait for prey. Common snappers have small eyes, and they rely on a keen sense of smell to find their prey. When a victim comes within range, the common snapper shoots out its long neck and grabs the prey in its jaws. Strong muscles in the snapper's large head mean that it has a powerful bite.

Common snapping turtles can be recognized by the saw-toothed edge of the back of their carapace. They eat fish, frogs, birds, small mammals, and lizards.

Hunted for soup

Freshwater turtles often have been hunted for their meat, especially for turtle soup. During the 1960s and 1970s, large companies hunted alligator snapper turtles for canned turtle soup. However, snapping turtles breed slowly, so overhunting quickly caused their numbers to fall. Today, alligator snappers are protected in most areas where they live.

Common snappers sometimes travel over land from one stream or lake to another, and females lay eggs on land. Out of the water they are aggressive, even toward humans, and may bite.

Alligator snappers

Alligator snapping turtles live only near the Mississippi River. Like common snappers, they ambush their prey. Alligator snappers eat fish, shellfish, smaller turtles, and birds. They also eat carrion (dead and rotting meat), which they find using their excellent sense of smell.

Alligator snappers hardly ever leave the water, except when the females lay their eggs. This happens in spring, about two months after mating. Females dig a nest in the soil just above the water line, and lay between 10 and 50 eggs. The eggs hatch 12 to 18 weeks later.

The pink object in an alligator snapper's mouth is part of its tongue. Alligator snappers do not have gills, so they must surface every twenty minutes to breathe.

Leatherback Turtle

The surface of the Pacific Ocean off the coast of Australia is dotted with what look like pinkish balloons. They are the gas-filled bodies of Portuguese men-of-war. The deadly tentacles of these jellyfish trail in the water to a depth of 164 feet (50 meters). A giant turtle surfaces next to this balloon-like creature and punctures it with a swift bite. The turtle then opens its mouth wide and sucks in the jellyfish, deadly tentacles and all.

Leatherback turtles are probably the most unusual of all turtles. These ocean-going giants are the biggest living turtles, with a length of up to 8 feet (2.4 meters). Leatherbacks get their name from their shell. Unlike the shell of any other turtle, it is leathery or rubbery, rather than hard and horny.

Living in the ocean

There are seven different kinds of sea turtle, but the leatherback is the one best adapted to ocean life. In all sea turtles the front legs are enlarged and flattened into paddle-like flippers. A leatherback's front flippers are the biggest. All sea turtles have streamlined shells, but the leathery, teardrop-shaped shell of the leatherback is especially good for slipping smoothly through the water.

Other sea turtles live mainly close to the coasts, but leatherbacks are true ocean travelers. They travel thousands of miles each year in search of their main prey—jellyfish.

The bony part of a leatherback's shell is made up of small, bony plates covered by a tough, leathery skin in place of the usual horny scales.

Box jellyfish are found mostly in the Gulf Stream in the Atlantic and in warmer parts of the Indian and Pacific oceans. They sometimes float in groups of thousands.

Stinging prey

Jellyfish are soft-bodied and seemingly defenseless, but most species have stinging tentacles that make most predators think twice before taking a mouthful. Some kinds of jellyfish, such as box jellyfish and the Portuguese man-of-war, have deadly stingers that can kill a human. However, leatherbacks eat even these deadly stingers. They are able to eat them because they have a special way of neutralizing jellyfish stingers in their stomach.

Jellyfish are not very nutritious, as they are mostly water, so leatherbacks need to eat large numbers of them to survive. In spring and summer, huge numbers of jellyfish gather in cooler waters, such as off the coast of Canada, Great Britain, or Japan. The leatherbacks travel to these areas to feed on the jellyfish. Leatherbacks catch their prey by swimming toward them and suddenly opening their mouth and throat. This sudden opening sucks the jellyfish into the leatherback's mouth.

Almost warm-blooded

Leatherbacks travel farther north and south than any other sea turtles in search of their prey. They can range as far north as Greenland and Iceland, where the sea temperature can be close to 32° F (0° C). Leatherbacks can survive at these temperatures because they have several ways of keeping their body warmer than the surrounding sea. They have a thick layer of fat below their skin, which insulates them from the cold. They also have a special system for warming up the cold blood coming back into their body from the flippers.

Deep divers

Although they live in the oceans, leatherbacks do not have gills, and they have to come to the surface regularly to breathe. Some kinds of jellyfish spend the day hundreds of feet below the surface, then come up into shallower water at night to feed. Researchers have found that leatherbacks can dive to depths of up to 3,280 feet (1,000 meters) in order to feed on these jellyfish. To do this they have to hold their breath for longer than half an hour. The leatherback's flexible shell is thought to be important in allowing the turtle to dive to such depths.

This leatherback turtle is trapped in fishing lines. Conservationists are working to save leatherbacks by protecting their nesting beaches and trying to change fishing methods.

Coming to land

Like all sea turtles, leatherbacks mate at sea, but they lay their eggs on land. Every two or three years, female leatherbacks swim to the beach where they were hatched to lay eggs. They dig a hole in the sand, lay about 80 round eggs, and then cover them up with sand.

The eggs hatch just over two months later, and the young turtles dig their way up to the surface. When it is dark, all the hatchlings head for the sea as fast as they can. Many are killed and eaten on the beach or in the shallower water close to land. Scientists estimate that only one hatchling in a thousand survives to become an adult. Leatherbacks are old enough to mate at 10 to 15 years old, and they live for up to 50 years.

The trip from the nest to the ocean is the most dangerous of the leatherback's life. Crabs, birds, and other predators kill large numbers in this short trip.

Disappearing leatherbacks

Since the 1980s, the numbers of female leatherbacks have fallen dramatically. In 1982 there were about 115,000 females, but by 2004 there were estimated to be fewer than 30,000. Leatherbacks are now the most seriously endangered of all sea turtles. The reasons for this rapid fall are not fully understood. One cause is thought to be that turtles are caught and killed accidentally by longline fishing boats. Some turtles also die from eating plastic bags and deflated balloons, which they mistake for jellyfish.

Lizards

In a house in southern Pakistan a moth flutters around the electric light. It crashes into the light bulb several times, then rests briefly on the ceiling. It lands close to a small lizard, frozen motionless in a shadowy corner of the room. The lizard suddenly comes to life, running quickly across the ceiling to grab the resting moth in its mouth.

In tropical countries, geckos are a common sight in many homes. People do not mind them running over the walls and ceiling because they catch mosquitoes, flies, and other insects. Geckos, iguanas, chameleons, monitors, and slow worms are just a few of the huge variety of lizards. In warmer regions there are lizards everywhere, from desert sand dunes to the tops of rain forest trees. There are fewer lizards in cooler climates, but they live as far north as Canada and as far south as the southern tip of South America.

From four legs to no legs

Lizards are far more varied than turtles, crocodiles, or snakes. There are long-legged lizards, short-legged lizards, and lizards with no legs at all. There are smooth, sleek lizards, lizards covered in prickly thorns, lizards with

There are more than 4,500 different kinds of lizards—more than half of all reptile species. Only a few, such as this tokay lizard, hunt prey larger than insects.

Australia's frilled lizard has one of the most extravagant frills of any lizard. It spreads its frill to make itself look bigger if threatened.

frills, and lizards with horns or with bony helmets. There are lizards that swim in sand, lizards that glide through the air, and even lizards that walk on water. Nearly all of these thousands of different lizards eat other animals.

From insects to buffalo

Many lizards are small and eat prey such as insects. Others are omnivores that eat both plants and animals. A few larger lizards eat bigger prey. Snake lizards from Australia hunt at night for other lizards and for snakes. Large geckos, called tokays, hunt lizards, small mammals, and birds. The largest lizard of all, the Komodo dragon, hunts deer, pigs, and even water buffalo. Komodo dragons also eat carrion.

Hunting senses

Some lizards sit and wait for their prey, while others actively look for victims. Most lizards have good eyesight, and this is often their main sense used for finding prey. Night hunters such as geckos have very large eyes, to gather as much light as possible, but they also have excellent hearing. Many lizards also have a good sense of smell.

Lizards are among the most successful survivors in desert regions. Sand fish spend most of their time swimming through sand dunes, hunting prey such as insect larvae.

15

Chameleon

On a thin branch in a Madagascar forest, a chameleon's green body blends in with the leaves around it. On a twig 12 inches (30 centimeters) away, a small bird perches, unaware of the chameleon close by. The chameleon opens its mouth, and in a split second shoots out its long tongue. The end of its tongue hits the bird and sticks to it. The chameleon pulls its tongue in again, with the bird still held tightly on the tip.

Chameleons are slow-moving lizards designed for life in the trees. Most chameleons live in Africa, south of the Sahara desert, or on the island of Madagascar. There are also chameleon species in Spain, North Africa, India, and the Middle East. They are best known for their long tongues and amazing color-changing abilities.

Made for the trees

More than perhaps any other lizards, chameleons are designed for life in the trees. Their bodies are long and flat, which makes it easier for them to balance on thin branches. Their toes are like pairs of pincers, designed for gripping branches rather than walking on the ground. A chameleon's tail is prehensile, meaning that it can grip branches or other objects. When not in use, the chameleon keeps its tail curled in a spiral.

Many chameleons have a kind of helmet (called a casque) on their head, as well as a ridge down their back.

Slow-motion hunters

All chameleons eat insects, but some also eat larger prey such as birds or other lizards. They are solitary hunters that move slowly through the branches looking for prey, or stand motionless waiting for an animal to come along.

Chameleons have a poor sense of smell and they can hear only low sounds. They rely almost entirely on their eyesight to find and catch their prey.

A chameleon's eyes are unlike those of any other animal. The bulging eyes are almost completely covered with skin, with only a small gap in front of each pupil to let in light. Each eye can move independently of the other. One eye can be scanning the branches below for prey while the other eye is watching the sky above for predators. However, when a chameleon spots prey, both eyes focus on it. With both eyes on the target, the chameleon can judge the distance accurately, and it gets ready to unleash its tongue.

A chameleon's eyes are like two telephoto lenses that magnify small areas of their surroundings.

An amazing tongue

Although a chameleon moves slowly, its tongue can move very fast. At the back of the mouth the tongue is fastened to a bone. To shoot the tongue out, muscles squeeze against this bone and move the tongue forward. It is similar to squeezing a bar of slippery soap, which then shoots out of your hands. The tip of a chameleon's tongue is sticky, and it can also grip the prey. Once the tongue reaches its target, another set of muscles comes into action and pulls the tongue back into the mouth.

Changing color

Chameleons are famous for being able to change color. The normal color of many chameleons is green or brownish—colors that give them good camouflage in trees. They can change color for several different reasons. In the mornings chameleons are often a dark color, to help them warm up more quickly (dark colors absorb heat better than light colors). As the sun gets hot, chameleons often turn much lighter to prevent themselves from overheating.

Chameleons also use colors to communicate their mood. If they are excited, frightened, or angry their colors may darken, and the chameleons become more strongly patterned. When two male chameleons fight over a female, they may engage in a color-changing contest. The male that puts on the brightest color display is the winner. If a female chameleon wants to mate with a male she will display dull colors, but if she is brightly patterned this means she wants other chameleons to stay away.

Desert chameleons

Despite their pincer-like feet designed for holding on to branches, Namaqua chameleons live on the ground. They chase insect prey such as beetles, but they also catch larger and more dangerous prey such as scorpions and small snakes.

Eggs and young

Five or six weeks after mating, a female chameleon is ready to lay her eggs. Most chameleons come down from the trees and dig a hole in which they lay between 30 and 80 eggs. They then cover over the eggs with soil. Egg laying is very dangerous for the female as she is in danger from predators on the ground, and it can take several days to dig the hole. When the young hatch, they dig themselves out and head for the nearest tree or bush.

African dwarf chameleons do not lay eggs, but instead give birth to between five and ten live babies.

When two male panther chameleons from Madagascar are competing for a mate, they swell up and turn red and yellow.

Komodo Dragon

Astag moves along a path through the savanna on the island of Komodo, Indonesia. It stops and sniffs the air. There is some unknown danger. Before the deer can run, a huge lizard pops up from the grass only a few feet away. It hurls itself at the deer's back legs, slicing through the tendons with its razor-sharp teeth and bringing its victim crashing down.

Komodo dragons can reach a length of 10 feet (3 meters) and weigh over 220 pounds (100 kilograms), which makes them the world's largest lizards. They are found only on a few small islands in Indonesia. Komodo dragons belong to a group known as the monitor lizards.

Fierce weapons

Komodo dragons have an impressive armory of weapons. They have more than 50 sharp, backward-curving teeth, which are ideal for slicing through flesh. A Komodo dragon's teeth stay sharp because they are always being replaced. Each tooth lasts only about three months.

As well as their teeth, Komodo dragons have powerful front legs equipped with curved, razor-sharp claws for holding down prey or ripping through flesh. A dragon can also deliver a vicious blow with its tail.

Hunting large prey

Komodo dragons hunt larger prey than other lizards. Their most common victims are deer, goats, and wild boar, but they sometimes kill buffalo weighing up to 1,320 pounds (600 kilograms).

A Komodo dragon's teeth are sharp on the back edge, which is good for slicing through flesh. Most of the teeth have a saw-toothed cutting edge.

Poisonous lizards

Only two kinds of lizard are poisonous—the Gila monster and its close relative, the Mexican beaded lizard. They are not monitor lizards but close cousins. Both species live in dry, hot regions in the southwestern United States and Mexico. Poison glands in the lower jaw are connected to the teeth, which have grooves that allow venom to flow down them. Although a Gila monster can give a human a very painful bite, it rarely causes death. The lizard has to chew poison into the bite for several minutes to cause real harm.

Like most lizards, Komodo dragons have good eyesight, but they usually find food using their excellent sense of smell. Often they lie in wait beside a trail used by prey animals. When an animal comes along, the Komodo dragon bursts out and ambushes it. With smaller prey, the dragon will grab its neck, back, or legs and throw it to the ground. The dragon then slashes open its victim's belly with its claws. With larger prey, the dragon will first bite the tendons in the legs. This leaves the animal unable to defend itself.

Monitor lizards are found in Australia, southern Asia, and Africa. Many of them are large lizards like this water monitor, and most are predators.

A deadly bite

Even if a Komodo dragon is unable to complete its attack and manages only a single bite, it may still succeed in killing its prey. Komodo dragons are not poisonous, but their mouths contain large numbers of disease-causing bacteria. In many cases the wound caused by a bite quickly becomes infected, and the injured animal dies within a few days. The smell of the dead carcass soon leads Komodo dragons to the spot.

As well as killing fresh prey, Komodo dragons also eat carrion. Komodo dragons generally live and hunt alone, but when a large animal dies the smell usually attracts several lizards. They devour the body quickly, ripping off large pieces of meat. A hungry Komodo dragon can eat a wild boar or similarly sized animal in about fifteen minutes. It eats nearly the whole animal, including the hair and bones. However, several hours after a meal it will regurgitate (bring up) a large pellet containing hair, pieces of bone, and other parts that are hard to digest.

A Komodo dragon's extremely sensitive sense of smell means that it can scent rotting meat from a distance of several miles.

Once they have laid their eggs, female Komodo dragons do not care for them in any way. Many young Komodo dragons are eaten by other adult Komodo dragons.

Mating and eggs

Male and female Komodo dragons often mate near a large carcass, because this is the only place where dragons meet. A few weeks after successful mating, the female is ready to lay eggs. She digs a pit in the ground and lays up to 25 eggs in one batch.

The eggs hatch after about eight to nine months. The hatchlings are thin, active lizards between 9 to 21 inches (22 and 55 centimeters) long. At first they hunt insects, but later they move on to rodents, birds, and other small prey. By five to seven years old, they are fully adult and able to mate, but they continue to grow all their lives. In the wild, Komodo dragons live to a maximum age of about 40 years old.

Prehistoric giants

Some prehistoric monitor lizards were much bigger than Komodo dragons. An extinct monitor lizard called Megalania was the largest lizard ever known. It lived in Australia as recently as 20,000 years ago, feeding on giant kangaroos, wombats, and other plant eaters of the time. Scientists have found fossils of Megalania that show it grew to a length of 23 feet (7 meters) or more.

Crocs and Alligators

In the waters of a murky lake in Africa, a crocodile lies motionless. It cannot see far in the cloudy water, but it does not need to. Pressure sensors around its mouth pick up the ripples that fish make as they swim. One fish swims close to the croc, setting off a wave of messages in the croc's pressure sensors. The croc reacts with a snap of its huge jaws.

Crocodilians (crocodiles and alligators) are found in warm rivers, lakes, and swamps around the world. There are also crocodilians in the oceans, and even some in the desert! They have been the top predators in water for 200 million years.

Crocodile groups

All crocodilians look broadly similar. They have a long body, a long tail, short legs, and a large head with elongated jaws. A crocodilian's back is ridged and often has bony armor under the skin.

Crocodilians are divided into three groups—crocodiles, alligators, and gharials (sometimes called gavials). There is only one species of gharial, a fish-eating crocodilian with a thin snout. The alligator family consists of alligators and caimans (Central and South American alligators).

A crocodilian's huge jaws contain pointed teeth. The croc can close its jaws with a force of about a ton, which is enough to crush an animal's skull with ease.

Although crocodiles move quite well on land, they are most at home in water. Its tail supplies the power for swimming, while its legs help steer and stop the croc from turning over.

Telling crocodiles from alligators

Alligators look similar to crocodiles, but there are a couple of important differences. Alligators have a very broad snout, and when an alligator's mouth is closed, its teeth are all hidden. A crocodile's snout is narrower, and one pair of teeth shows even when its mouth is closed.

Water hunters

Crocodilians are well adapted to ambushing prey in the water. Their eyes and nostrils are set on the very top of their head, so that they can lie with just their eyes and nose showing above water. They can also dive for fifteen minutes or more without difficulty. Crocodilians use their muscular tails to power them through the water. A crocodilian's main weapons are its huge jaws. It can also use its powerful tail to stun an animal or knock it over.

Super croc!

About 110 million years ago, a 39-foot (12-meter) crocodilian lived in the rivers of northern Africa. This super croc was almost twice as long as the biggest crocs alive today and weighed nearly ten times as much. Its prey are thought to have included dinosaurs.

An almost complete fossil skeleton of the supercroc (*Sarcosuchus imperator*) was found in the Sahara Desert. It was as long as a bus and weighed ten tons.

Nile Crocodile

In eastern Africa, thousands of migrating wildebeest are crossing the Talek River. They cross at the same place every year. The crossing place is a gathering place for crocodiles, too. The crocs cruise through the water, taking their time to pick a wildebeest that is slower or weaker than the rest. In the deepest part of the river they attack, dragging their victim to its death.

Despite their name, Nile crocodiles live in rivers throughout Africa. They also live in marshes and swamps, and sometimes on the coast. Nile crocodiles can grow to a length of 16 feet (5.5 meters). They can kill animals as large as buffalo, and sometimes they kill humans.

Ambush hunters

Nile crocodiles will eat almost any prey they can catch and overpower. Smaller crocs eat mostly fish, but they also catch water birds, frogs, snakes, turtles, and rats. The biggest crocs eat this prey, too, but they also hunt large mammals, such as antelopes, zebras, monkeys, sheep, goats, and even water buffalo and hippopotamuses.

Nile crocodiles hunt in various ways, but most often they lie in wait for their prey. When catching fish, they grab their victims with a quick sideways snap of the jaws.

The favorite hunting place for Nile crocodiles is the water's edge. Here they can grab land animals that come down to the water to drink.

Nile crocodiles are the largest, and probably also the most common, large predators in Africa.

Tackling large prey

Nile crocodiles have several ways of dealing with larger land mammals. They often grab animals such as antelopes by the head and drag them into the water, then hold them under to drown them. With larger, stronger prey, the croc will usually try to throw the animal off its feet before hauling it into the water.

A crocodile's teeth cannot slice or chew, so if its prey is too large to swallow whole, tearing it into bite-sized pieces can be a problem. Nile crocs get around this by grabbing hold of a leg or a chunk of flesh and then spinning themselves in the water to twist it off.

Eating stones

Crocodiles sometimes deliberately swallow stones or other hard objects as large as a fist. At one time scientists thought that crocodiles needed the stones to help them dive. However, researchers have found that the middle part of a crocodile's stomach acts like a grinding machine. The stones in its stomach help break up bones and grind up meat.

Social crocs

Nile crocodiles are more social than most crocs. Groups of adult crocodiles often bask in the sun together in the mornings, while younger crocodiles usually live in groups of two or three. One very large male usually dominates the adult group.

Nile crocodiles also sometimes hunt in groups. Groups of Nile crocodiles gather at crossing points where herds of antelopes or wildebeest cross rivers on their annual migrations. The crocs usually hunt for themselves, but if one of them catches a large animal, others will gather and tear at the victim. This does not usually result in fighting between the crocodiles because the prey animal is big enough to feed several crocs, and the carcass is difficult for a single croc to tear apart.

On some occasions, Nile crocodiles really do cooperate to catch prey. Each year, large schools of mullet swim into Lake St. Lucia in southern Africa to breed. During these annual migrations, groups of crocodiles gather at a narrow part of the lake and spread themselves across in a line. Each crocodile snaps up fish that swim close by, but it stays in its place in the line so that there are no gaps where the mullet can slip through.

Crocodile toothbrush

Even large crocodiles will snap up a bird as a snack, but the crocodile bird is safe from a croc's jaws. These birds hop around on the crocodile's skin, snapping up any parasites that they find. The birds even hop into the croc's open mouth to pick out leeches and pieces of food.

Nesting and young

Female crocodiles usually mate with the dominant male in their group. About 60 days later the female digs a hole in the ground where she lays between 20 and 80 eggs. Nesting sites are usually in sandy soil close to the river, but high enough to avoid flooding. At the best nesting sites there are often several nests quite close together.

Most reptiles take no care of their eggs, but crocodilians are different. Female Nile crocodiles guard their nests throughout the time it takes the eggs to develop (about twelve weeks). Once the young crocodiles start to hatch they call from inside the nest, and the mother digs it up. She then carries the hatchlings in her mouth to a quiet stretch of water. The hatchlings stay in a group, guarded by their mother, for several weeks after hatching.

Nile crocodiles can hunt almost as soon as they hatch. They begin by hunting insects and then move on to frogs, crabs, and young fish.

29

Saltwater Crocodile

On a cruise ship in northern Australia, a tour guide holds a piece of meat high over the water on a long pole. Soon a saltwater crocodile comes alongside the boat. With a tremendous surge the croc lunges out of the water, its back legs clearing the surface as it leaps. With one snap of its jaws, the meat is gone.

Saltwater crocodiles (called salties) are found in the ocean, in mangrove swamps, and in rivers from India to northern Australia. They are the biggest of all crocodilians – in fact, they are the largest living reptiles. They can be up to 23 feet (7 meters) long and weigh 2,200 pounds (1000 kilograms).

Getting rid of salt

One problem for land animals that spend most of their time in salt water is that sea water is too salty to drink. The salt sucks water out of the animal's body, and will eventually cause death.

Saltwater crocodiles do not have this problem because special glands on their tongue get rid of excess salt. Other crocodiles have similar salt glands, despite the fact that most live in fresh water.

Despite their size, saltwater crocodiles are tremendously agile.

Unfussy feeders

Salties catch a wide variety of foods, from insects and frogs to large mammals. Big salties feed on large prey, including deer, wild boar, kangaroos, and buffalo. Like Nile crocodiles, they sometimes kill and eat humans.

Even very large salties eat smaller prey as well as larger animals. They often lie in mangrove swamps beneath colonies of fruit bats, for instance, and catch bats that come down to drink. They can also grab birds or bats sitting on low perches, by pushing themselves out of the water with their tails.

Saltwater crocodiles kill larger prey in a similar way to Nile crocodiles, first overpowering them or knocking them down, and then dragging them underwater.

A narrow escape

In 1981 Hilton Graham took twelve-year-old Peta-Lynn Mann on a boat trip in the swamps near Darwin, Australia. Hilton dropped his gun in shallow water, and while he was trying to get it back he was attacked by a thirteen-foot (four-meter) saltwater crocodile. With Peta-Lynn's help Hilton managed to stop the croc from dragging him underwater, but he was badly injured. Although she was only twelve, Peta-Lynn managed to phone for help and drive Hilton to safety in a truck.

Male saltwater crocodiles can sometimes scare off rivals for their territory with aggressive displays, but other times they fight by ramming their heads together.

Mating and nests

Male saltwater crocodiles are territorial, meaning that they defend the area where they live (their territory) from other males. Only large, powerful males can keep a territory. Weaker males are thrown out by stronger ones.

Fighting to defend territories is most violent at the start of the wet season, because this is the time when males and females mate. Females are much more likely to mate with a male if he has a territory.

Instead of digging a hole for a nest, female salties build a mound nest made of soil and plants. Females lay their eggs (usually 40 to 60 of them) in a hollow in the center of the mound, and then cover them with soil.

Hatching

Like Nile crocodiles, female salties keep watch on their eggs and chase away nest robbers such as monitor lizards and wild pigs. As the plant material in the nest rots, it gives off heat and warms the nest mound, similar to a compost heap. This helps keep the eggs at the right temperature. If the nest gets too hot and the eggs are in danger of overheating, the female will throw water on the mound to cool it down.

When the eggs are ready to hatch, the baby crocodiles begin to call out. The female breaks open the mound to release the hatchlings, and then she carries them in her mouth to a quiet stretch of water. The female continues to guard the hatchlings for several months after they are born.

Farmed for their skins

Saltwater crocodiles are highly valued for their skins. Unlike other crocodile skins, theirs have very little bony armor in them. From 1945 to 1970, salties were widely hunted for their skins, and crocodile populations fell dramatically. However, since the 1970s, saltwater crocodiles have been protected in many countries where they live. Instead of killing wild animals for their skins, saltwater crocodiles are now raised on crocodile farms.

Male or female?

The temperature at which the eggs incubate is important, because it affects whether the crocs that hatch are male or female. In mammals, birds, and many other animals, the sex of a baby is decided at the very start of its development. However, in crocodilians and some other reptiles, temperature affects whether an egg hatches as a male or a female. In salties, if the eggs incubate at about 90° F (32° C) they will hatch as males, but above or below that temperature, they are more likely to be females.

Like Nile crocodiles, female salties protect their eggs. The eggs take about three months to hatch. Fewer than 1 in 100 hatchlings makes it to adulthood.

33

Australian Freshwater Crocodile

It is summer, the wet season in northern Australia. In the McKinley River, an Australian freshwater crocodile swims along slowly, close to the bank. Its tail is curved inwards, stirring up the water as it swims. Groups of small fish sheltering under the bank dart away to escape the croc's tail. Many swim straight toward the freshwater crocodile's jaws, and the croc snaps them up.

Australian freshwater crocodiles live in rivers and streams in northern Australia. They are fairly small crocodiles. Males grow no bigger than 8 feet (2.5 meters) long, while females rarely get bigger than 6.5 feet (2 meters).

Fish specialists

Australian freshwater crocodiles eat a range of fairly small prey, including frogs, lizards, small mammals, and birds. However, their main prey are fish. Australian freshwater crocodiles have a slender snout, which is more effective for catching fish. Crocodilians usually catch fish by snapping them up with a sideways movement, as this is quicker than trying to lunge forward when attacking. A thin snout is better

Australian freshwater crocodiles are agile on land as well as in the water. Unlike most other crocs, they can run. If they are in a real hurry, they can zoom along for short distances at a bounding gallop.

Like other crocs, the Australian freshwater crocodile swallows fish head first, to avoid the scales catching in its throat.

for this because it can move sideways through the water more easily.

Another way that Australian freshwater crocodiles hunt is by lying in the shallow water near the shore and attacking animals that come to drink. They can also leap almost completely out of the water to catch perching birds.

Getting through the dry season

During the dry season, water is scarce and prey is much harder for freshwater crocodiles to find. In the lower parts of rivers the crocs shelter from the heat in deep billabongs, or pools. They eat very little, surviving on fat reserves stored in their tails.

Farther upstream, some rivers dry out completely. In these areas Australian freshwater crocodiles dig burrows and lie dormant until the rains arrive.

Nesting and young

Like Nile crocodiles, female freshwater crocs dig a pit where they lay their eggs. The females guard the eggs while they develop, and dig out the young when they begin to hatch. They also look after their young for about a month after hatching.

Not just in freshwater

In the 1950s and 1960s saltwater crocodiles were overhunted and their numbers fell. During this time Australian freshwater crocodiles spread farther downstream and took over some of the salties' coastal habitats. When saltie hunting was controlled in the 1970s and 1980s, numbers of saltwater crocodiles rose again and freshwater crocodiles were pushed back upstream.

American Alligator

It is the height of summer in Florida, and some of the alligator holes, where American alligators shelter from the heat, are drying out. One alligator is searching for a new home in a Miami suburb. It spent the previous night in a swimming pool, and now it is walking across a golf course, heading for the water hazard.

American alligators are the best-known members of the alligator family. In the past they lived across the southern United States, but today much of their swampy or marshy habitat has been drained and built on. American alligators are now found mainly in parts of Louisiana and Florida. The largest grow to a length of about 13 feet (4 meters).

Swamp hunters

American alligators usually live in swampy or marshy areas. The long reeds and other vegetation provide plenty of places for the alligator to lie concealed and wait for prey.

American alligators feed on almost anything they can catch. This is mostly small prey such as catfish, mice, rats, nutria (a kind of rodent), bullfrogs, ducks, egrets, herons, and turtles. An alligator's broad jaws are powerful enough to crush even the strongest turtle shells.

Alligators rely on stealth to catch their prey—for instance, lying in the reeds by a drinking place or swimming quietly beneath a water bird and grabbing it from below. As with other crocodilians, they are surprisingly agile for such large animals. They can leap 6.5 feet (2 meters) out of the water to snatch a bird from its perch.

Wild American alligators were hunted in the past for their skin and meat. Today, alligator farms provide skins and meat without reducing wild alligator populations.

In the Everglades National Park in Florida, American alligators and their habitat are protected.

North of the Tropics

The American alligator lives farther from the warm Tropics than other crocodilians. In winter, ponds and lakes can freeze over, while in summer it can be so hot that many pools and ponds dry out.

American alligators survive the cold by lying dormant. They dig burrows consisting of a tunnel leading to a larger chamber. Here the alligator lies resting for up to four months.

Crocodilian teeth

A crocodilian's teeth are its main weapons, and they suffer a lot of wear and tear. Each tooth lasts an average of only about a year, although teeth at the back of the mouth last longer than those at the front. Crocs and alligators always have a full set of teeth because worn teeth are continually being replaced. Each of the crocodilian's current teeth has a cavity (hole) underneath it where the next tooth begins to grow. This means that when a tooth falls out, there is already a well-grown new one ready to take its place.

As more and more of their natural habitat is drained or built on, wild alligators find their way into towns and cities.

Surviving cold and heat

American alligators can survive a short cold spell outside the shelter of a burrow. They lie in shallow water with their body underwater and their nostrils above the surface. If the water at the surface freezes, warm air from the alligator's nostrils keeps a hole open in the ice.

In hot weather, alligators need to lie in water to avoid overheating. To make sure that they have water even when shallow pools dry up, American alligators dig alligator holes up to 26 feet (8 meters) across, which are deep enough to have water in them even in dry weather.

Finding a mate

In early spring, just after they wake from their winter hibernation, American alligators find partners and mate. At this time of year glands in the tail of both male and female alligators produce a distinctive scent.

Female American alligators begin to build their nests in early June. Like saltwater crocodiles, they build mound nests. After building up a pile of vegetation and soil, the female digs a hollow in the top in which she lays 30 or more eggs.

The female alligator guards the nest for most of the nine or ten weeks it takes for the eggs to develop. She only leaves the nest briefly to look for food. Despite the female's care, about a fifth of the nests are robbed by raccoons or black bears.

Alligator holes provide a refuge for other wild animals as well as for alligators themselves.

Female alligators do most of their nest building at night. As with other crocodilians, the mother guards her hatchlings for several weeks after they hatch.

Hatching and young

The eggs hatch between late July and September. The new hatchlings soon begin to hunt for food, usually insects or other small creatures. While they are small they are vulnerable to attack from predators such as blue herons. If attacked they make a distress call, which brings the nearest adult alligator charging to the rescue.

American alligators are not fully adult until about five years of age. Females may begin to breed at this age, but a male may be fifteen years old before he is large enough to defend a female from rival males.

Chinese alligators

Although they live on the other side of the world, Chinese alligators are the closest relatives of American alligators. These alligators grow to only about 5 feet (1.5 meters), and they dig large underground burrows where they can hide away from people. These burrows have enabled small groups of alligators to survive, but they are isolated from each other by populated areas. Unless great efforts are made to save them, Chinese alligators will soon become extinct in the wild.

Black Caiman

It is late evening in the grasslands of Brazil. A group of capybaras are feeding quietly close to a lake. A black caiman on the lake shore picks up the sounds of the capybaras feeding and creeps silently towards them. With its excellent night vision it can see the capybaras clearly. The caiman picks a victim and charges straight toward it, moving fast. The capybara turns to flee, but the caiman's jaws close around it before it can run.

Black caimans are the largest South American reptiles. The largest black caimans are bigger than American alligators. They can grow to 20 feet (6 meters) or so in length. Black caimans live in grasslands, forests, and areas that flood in the wet season each year.

Equipped for night hunting

Black caimans hunt mainly at night, and their senses are finely tuned for night hunting. They have keen hearing, and although all crocodiles have good night vision, a black caiman's eyes are particularly sensitive to dim light.

Like other crocodilians, black caimans eat a wide range of prey. They hunt fish, including catfish and piranhas, but they also attack a range of land animals. Capybaras are a favorite prey for large black caimans. They also sometimes kill and eat domestic cattle.

Black caimans look similar to American alligators, but they are more closely related to other caimans. Like most caimans they have a bony ridge over their eyes.

Hunted for skins

Like most crocodilians, black caimans were hunted for much of the 20th century for their skins. By the 1970s, populations of black caimans had been reduced to just one hundredth of their numbers a century earlier.

Juvenile black caimans have pale yellow, white, and gray bands on their head and body. These bands gradually fade as they get older.

In many areas black caimans disappeared altogether, and this disappearance had several unexpected effects. Without caimans to keep them in check, the numbers of capybaras rose, and they began to eat farm crops. Numbers of piranhas also increased, and they became a danger for cattle in flooded grasslands.

Black caimans are now protected in most countries where they are found, and in some areas their numbers have recovered well. In some areas they are killed illegally for meat, but their future looks more hopeful than it did in the 1970s.

Dwarf caimans

Schneider's dwarf caiman is a small caiman found only in South American rain forests. These caimans grow to just over 5 feet (1.5 meters) long. On the cool rain forest floor, it is hard for females to keep their eggs warm enough to hatch. So dwarf caimans often build their nests around termite mounds. The heat generated by the millions of termites living in the mound helps to keep the eggs at the right temperature.

Gharial

A gharial hangs almost motionless in a fast-flowing stretch of the Indus River in Pakistan. Its thin shape means that it needs very little effort to hold itself still in the rushing water. After a long wait, a school of fish swims by. The gharial strikes sideways, sometimes catching several fish at a time.

Gharials can grow as large as saltwater crocodiles, but they look very different from salties. A gharial's snout is long, thin, and flat. The snout of the adult male gharial has a large swelling on the end. Gharials live in rivers and streams in India and Pakistan. Unlike most crocodilians they prefer deep, fast-moving water.

The long snout and bulbous, nose-like snout end of a male gharial are unmistakable. This nose does not develop until the gharial is about ten years old.

Expert at fishing

More than any other crocodilians, gharials are designed for catching fish. Gharials have over 100 slender, needle-sharp teeth that point slightly outward. The teeth in the upper and lower jaws fit together when the mouth is closed, These thin, pointed teeth are ideal for holding on to slippery fish prey.

The gharial's thin jaws are designed for catching fish, too. The flattened snout slides easily through the water in the sideways snapping movement that all crocodilians use to catch fish.

Courtship and mating

Late winter is the time when gharials find partners and mate. Large male gharials gather and defend breeding groups of three or four females. They attract females by making loud buzzing and whistling noises. The bulb on the end of their snout is important for making these buzzing and whistling sounds.

Gharials spend much of their time basking in the sun on sandbanks. This is particularly important in the dry, cooler winter months.

Nesting and young

A month or so after mating, females begin nesting. The nest is usually a hole dug in a sandy riverbank. Females dig several test holes before laying about 40 eggs in the actual nest hole.

As with other crocodilians, the female guards the nest while the eggs develop. Males may also help with nest guarding. When the young hatch, the female leads them to a nearby stretch of water. She does not pick the hatchlings up because her snout is too narrow and her teeth are too sharp.

For the first few weeks the hatchlings stay together in a nursery group, guarded by the female or sometimes the male. Flooding caused by the monsoon rains breaks up the nursery groups after a few weeks.

Good for fishing

Catfish are among the gharial's most common prey. Catfish eat smaller fish called tilapia, which are an important part of the catch of local fishers. By keeping catfish numbers down, gharials help preserve tilapia stocks.

False gharials live in Southeast Asia. They were thought to belong to the crocodile family, but they may actually be relations of true gharials.

Classification Chart

Scientists classify living things (sort them into groups) by comparing their characteristics (their similarities and differences). A species is a group of animals or plants that are all similar and can breed together to produce young. Similar species are organized into a larger group called a genus (plural genera). Similar genera are grouped into families, and so on through bigger and bigger groupings—classes, orders, phyla, and kingdoms.

Turtles, lizards, and crocs are all reptiles: they belong to the class Reptilia. There are many reptile families, so reptiles are divided into several larger groups called subclasses. Turtles and tortoises form the subclass Chelonia, lizards and snakes together form the large subclass Squamata, and crocodilians form the subclass Crocodylia.

Subclass	Families	Genera/ species	Examples
Chelonia	14	99 genera, 293 species	sea turtles, leatherback turtle, pond turtles, tortoises
Squamata	20	442 genera, 4,560 species	chameleons, anoles, geckos, skinks, beaded lizards, monitor lizards
Crocodylia	3	8 genera, 23 species	Nile crocodile, American alligator, black caiman, gharial

Where Reptiles Live

This map shows where some of the reptiles in this book live.

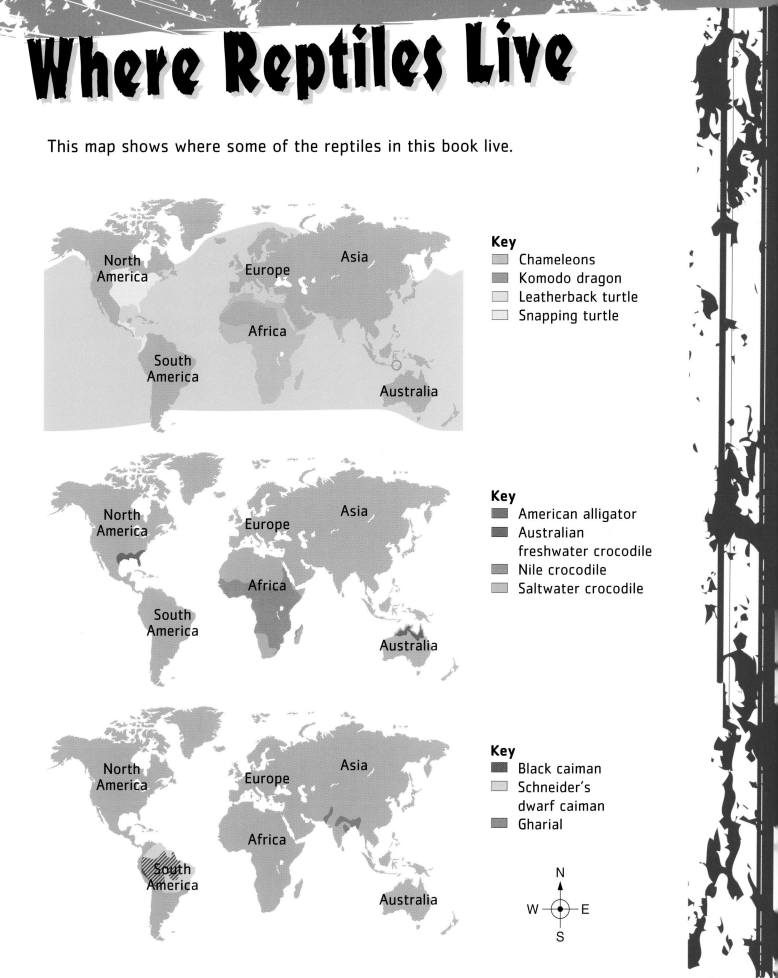

Key
- Chameleons
- Komodo dragon
- Leatherback turtle
- Snapping turtle

Key
- American alligator
- Australian freshwater crocodile
- Nile crocodile
- Saltwater crocodile

Key
- Black caiman
- Schneider's dwarf caiman
- Gharial

Glossary

adapted way that a living thing has changed to fit in with its environment

ambush make a surprise attack from hiding

bacterium (plural bacteria) kind of very tiny living thing. Many bacteria are useful to us, but a few kinds cause disease

billabong backwater or pool on an Australian river

breed when animals mate and produce young

camouflage coloring and markings on an animal that help it blend in with its environment

capybara largest living rodent. The capybara looks like a giant guinea pig and is found in South America.

carapace top part of a tortoise or turtle's shell

carcass body of a dead animal

carrion dead and rotting meat

chelonian tortoise, turtle, or terrapin

class group of closely related families of living things

digest break down food so that the body can extract nutrients from it

dominate be the most powerful or important

dormant resting; not active

extinct when a whole group of living things dies out

family group of closely related genera of living things

fossil remains of an organism that have been preserved in the earth

genus (plural genera) group of species of living things that are closely related

gland organ in the body that produces substances such as tears, saliva, or venom

habitat place where an animal lives

larva (plural larvae) young stage of an insect

longline fishing fishing using a very long line with thousands of baited hooks

mammal hairy, warm-blooded animal that feeds its young on breast milk

mate when a male and a female animal come together to produce young

migrate travel a long way regularly each year

monsoon wind that brings rain to India and Southeast Asia each year

mullet fish that swims in large groups and is caught for food

neutralize make something harmless

omnivore animal that eats both animals and plants

order group of closely related classes of living things

parasite creature that lives on or in another living creature and takes food from it without giving any benefit in return

piranha fierce kind of predatory fish found in South American rivers

plastron bottom part of a turtle or tortoise's shell

predator animal that hunts and eats other animals

prehensile able to grasp like a hand

prey animal that is hunted by other animals

pupil dark spot in the center of the eye that lets in light

savanna grassland with scattered bushes and trees

species group of animals that are similar and can breed together to produce healthy offspring

streamlined having a smooth shape to slip easily through the water or air

tendon tough cord connecting muscle to bone

territory area where an animal lives and hunts. It defends this area from other animals.

Tropics/tropical land close to the equator where the weather is warm all year

venom poison

vertebrate animal that has a backbone

Further Reading

Deiters, Erika and Jim Deiters. *Animals of the Rain Forest: Chameleons.* Chicago: Raintree, 2001.

Facklam, Margery and Alan Male. *Lizards Weird and Wonderful.* New York: Little, Brown, 2003.

Spilsbury, Louise and Richard Spilsbury. *Animals Under Threat: Alligator.* Chicago: Heinemann Library, 2004.

Waters, Jo. *The Wild Side of Pet Lizards.* Chicago: Raintree, 2004.

Index